50 Low-Sugar Dessert Recipes for Home

By: Kelly Johnson

Table of Contents

- Sugar-Free Berry Chia Seed Pudding
- Almond Flour Chocolate Chip Cookies
- Avocado Chocolate Mousse
- Lemon Blueberry Yogurt Parfait
- Dark Chocolate-Dipped Strawberries
- Coconut Flour Banana Bread
- No-Bake Peanut Butter Energy Balls
- Greek Yogurt with Mixed Berries
- Sugar-Free Apple Cinnamon Muffins
- Raspberry Almond Thumbprint Cookies
- Chocolate Avocado Truffles
- Vanilla Chia Pudding with Fresh Berries
- Low-Sugar Mango Sorbet
- Pumpkin Spice Energy Bites
- Cinnamon Baked Apples
- Sugar-Free Chocolate Pudding
- Almond Joy Protein Bars
- Keto Cheesecake Bites
- Blueberry Coconut Milk Ice Cream
- No-Bake Almond Butter Cups
- Vanilla Ricotta Stuffed Strawberries
- Sugar-Free Lemon Bars
- Chocolate Covered Almonds
- Blackberry Coconut Chia Seed Pudding
- Low-Sugar Oatmeal Cookies
- Pistachio Dark Chocolate Bark
- Peach and Raspberry Yogurt Popsicles
- Walnut and Date Energy Bites
- Berry and Greek Yogurt Frozen Bites
- Sugar-Free Lemon Sorbet
- Almond Flour Pumpkin Muffins
- Raspberry Coconut Chia Jam
- Chocolate Avocado Popsicles
- No-Bake Coconut Cashew Bars
- Low-Sugar Blueberry Cheesecake

- Cacao Nib and Coconut Energy Bites
- Lemon Poppy Seed Ricotta Cake
- Vanilla Almond Protein Bites
- Sugar-Free Apple Pie Bites
- Cocoa Dusted Almonds
- Keto Pumpkin Pie Fat Bombs
- Hazelnut Chocolate Protein Balls
- Strawberry Coconut Milk Panna Cotta
- Low-Sugar Carrot Cake Bites
- Mint Chocolate Avocado Ice Cream
- Sugar-Free Cherry Almond Granola Bars
- Coconut Lime Chia Seed Pudding
- Almond Flour Chocolate Zucchini Bread
- Vanilla Coconut Flour Cupcakes
- Sugar-Free Matcha Green Tea Ice Cream

Sugar-Free Berry Chia Seed Pudding

Ingredients:

- 1/4 cup chia seeds
- 1 cup unsweetened almond milk (or any milk of your choice)
- 1 teaspoon vanilla extract
- 1-2 tablespoons sugar substitute (like stevia or erythritol)
- 1 cup mixed berries (strawberries, blueberries, raspberries)

Instructions:

In a bowl, combine chia seeds, almond milk, vanilla extract, and sugar substitute. Stir well to combine.
Let the mixture sit for about 5 minutes and stir again to prevent clumping.
Cover the bowl and refrigerate the chia seed mixture for at least 2 hours or overnight, allowing it to thicken.
Before serving, give the chia pudding a good stir to ensure it has a smooth consistency.
Wash and prepare the mixed berries.
Layer the chia seed pudding and mixed berries in serving glasses or bowls.
Top with additional berries and a drizzle of sugar substitute if desired.
Enjoy this delicious and sugar-free Berry Chia Seed Pudding as a healthy and satisfying dessert or breakfast option!

Almond Flour Chocolate Chip Cookies

Ingredients:

- 2 cups almond flour
- 1/2 teaspoon baking soda
- 1/4 teaspoon salt
- 1/3 cup coconut oil, melted
- 1/4 cup maple syrup or any sugar substitute of your choice
- 1 large egg
- 1 teaspoon vanilla extract
- 1/2 cup sugar-free chocolate chips

Instructions:

Preheat your oven to 350°F (175°C) and line a baking sheet with parchment paper.
In a large bowl, whisk together almond flour, baking soda, and salt.
In a separate bowl, mix together melted coconut oil, maple syrup (or sugar substitute), egg, and vanilla extract.
Combine the wet ingredients with the dry ingredients and stir until well combined.
Fold in the sugar-free chocolate chips.
Scoop out tablespoon-sized portions of cookie dough and place them on the prepared baking sheet, leaving some space between each cookie.
Flatten each cookie slightly with the back of a spoon or your fingers.
Bake in the preheated oven for 10-12 minutes or until the edges are golden brown.
Allow the cookies to cool on the baking sheet for a few minutes before transferring them to a wire rack to cool completely.
Enjoy these Almond Flour Chocolate Chip Cookies as a delicious and low-carb treat!

Avocado Chocolate Mousse

Ingredients:

- 2 ripe avocados
- 1/2 cup unsweetened cocoa powder
- 1/2 cup almond milk or any milk of your choice
- 1/4 cup maple syrup or any sweetener of your choice
- 1 teaspoon vanilla extract
- Pinch of salt
- Optional toppings: whipped coconut cream, berries, or chopped nuts

Instructions:

Cut the avocados in half, remove the pit, and scoop out the flesh.

In a blender or food processor, combine the avocado flesh, cocoa powder, almond milk, maple syrup, vanilla extract, and a pinch of salt.

Blend the ingredients until smooth and creamy, scraping down the sides of the blender or food processor as needed.

Taste the mixture and adjust the sweetness if necessary by adding more maple syrup.

Once the avocado chocolate mousse is smooth and well-blended, transfer it to serving bowls or glasses.

Refrigerate for at least 30 minutes to allow the mousse to chill and set.

Before serving, add optional toppings such as whipped coconut cream, berries, or chopped nuts.

Enjoy this decadent and creamy Avocado Chocolate Mousse as a healthier alternative to traditional chocolate desserts!

Lemon Blueberry Yogurt Parfait

Ingredients:

- 1 cup Greek yogurt (unsweetened)
- 1 tablespoon honey or maple syrup (optional)
- 1 teaspoon lemon zest
- 1 tablespoon fresh lemon juice
- 1 cup fresh blueberries
- 1/2 cup granola (choose a low-sugar option or make your own)
- Fresh mint leaves for garnish (optional)

Instructions:

In a bowl, mix Greek yogurt with honey or maple syrup (if using), lemon zest, and fresh lemon juice. Adjust sweetness to your liking.
In serving glasses or bowls, layer the yogurt mixture with fresh blueberries.
Add a layer of granola on top of the blueberries.
Repeat the layers until you reach the top of the glass, finishing with a dollop of yogurt.
Garnish with additional blueberries and fresh mint leaves, if desired.
Serve immediately and enjoy this refreshing Lemon Blueberry Yogurt Parfait as a healthy and delightful breakfast or snack!

Dark Chocolate-Dipped Strawberries

Ingredients:

- Fresh strawberries, washed and dried
- Dark chocolate chips or chopped dark chocolate (70% cocoa or higher)
- 1 tablespoon coconut oil (optional)
- Chopped nuts, shredded coconut, or sprinkles (optional, for coating)

Instructions:

Line a baking sheet with parchment paper.
In a microwave-safe bowl or using a double boiler, melt the dark chocolate. If using the microwave, heat in 20-30 second intervals, stirring between each, until fully melted. If desired, add coconut oil to create a smoother chocolate coating.
Hold each strawberry by the stem and dip it into the melted chocolate, ensuring it's well coated.
Allow excess chocolate to drip off, or gently scrape the bottom against the edge of the bowl.
Optional: Roll the dipped strawberry in chopped nuts, shredded coconut, or sprinkles for added texture and flavor.
Place the dipped strawberries on the prepared baking sheet.
Allow the chocolate to set by placing the strawberries in the refrigerator for about 15-20 minutes.
Once the chocolate has hardened, transfer the dark chocolate-dipped strawberries to a serving plate.
Serve and enjoy these decadent Dark Chocolate-Dipped Strawberries as a delightful treat for any occasion!

Coconut Flour Banana Bread

Ingredients:

- 4 ripe bananas, mashed
- 4 large eggs
- 1/2 cup coconut oil, melted
- 1/2 cup coconut flour
- 1/4 cup almond flour
- 1 teaspoon baking soda
- 1 teaspoon vanilla extract
- 1/2 teaspoon cinnamon
- 1/4 teaspoon salt
- Optional add-ins: chopped nuts, chocolate chips, or shredded coconut

Instructions:

Preheat your oven to 350°F (175°C). Grease or line a loaf pan with parchment paper.
In a large bowl, mash the ripe bananas.
Add the eggs, melted coconut oil, and vanilla extract to the mashed bananas. Mix until well combined.
In a separate bowl, whisk together the coconut flour, almond flour, baking soda, cinnamon, and salt.
Gradually add the dry ingredients to the banana mixture, stirring until there are no lumps.
If desired, fold in chopped nuts, chocolate chips, or shredded coconut.
Pour the batter into the prepared loaf pan, spreading it evenly.
Bake in the preheated oven for 50-60 minutes, or until a toothpick inserted into the center comes out clean.
Allow the Coconut Flour Banana Bread to cool in the pan for 10 minutes before transferring it to a wire rack to cool completely.
Once cooled, slice and enjoy this delicious and gluten-free Coconut Flour Banana Bread!

No-Bake Peanut Butter Energy Balls

Ingredients:

- 1 cup old-fashioned oats
- 1/2 cup creamy peanut butter
- 1/3 cup honey or maple syrup
- 1 cup unsweetened shredded coconut
- 1/2 cup ground flaxseed
- 1 teaspoon vanilla extract
- 1/2 cup mini chocolate chips (optional)
- Pinch of salt

Instructions:

In a large mixing bowl, combine old-fashioned oats, peanut butter, honey or maple syrup, shredded coconut, ground flaxseed, vanilla extract, and a pinch of salt.
If using, fold in the mini chocolate chips.
Stir the mixture until well combined. If it seems too dry, you can add a bit more peanut butter or honey.
Place the bowl in the refrigerator for about 30 minutes to make the mixture easier to handle.
After chilling, take small portions of the mixture and roll them into bite-sized balls using your hands.
Place the energy balls on a parchment-lined tray or plate.
Refrigerate the energy balls for at least 1 hour to firm up.
Once chilled, transfer the No-Bake Peanut Butter Energy Balls to an airtight container for storage.
Enjoy these nutritious and energy-packed treats as a quick snack or on-the-go pick-me-up!

Greek Yogurt with Mixed Berries

Ingredients:

- 1 cup Greek yogurt (unsweetened)
- 1 tablespoon honey or maple syrup (optional, for sweetness)
- 1/2 cup fresh strawberries, sliced
- 1/2 cup fresh blueberries
- 1/2 cup fresh raspberries
- 1/4 cup granola (optional, for crunch)

Instructions:

In a bowl, mix the Greek yogurt with honey or maple syrup, if desired, for added sweetness.

Wash and prepare the fresh berries.

In serving bowls or glasses, layer the Greek yogurt with the mixed berries.

Top the yogurt and berries with granola for added crunch, if desired.

Drizzle with an additional teaspoon of honey or maple syrup if you prefer extra sweetness.

Serve immediately and enjoy this simple and delicious Greek Yogurt with Mixed Berries as a wholesome breakfast or snack!

Sugar-Free Apple Cinnamon Muffins

Ingredients:

- 2 cups almond flour
- 1/2 cup coconut flour
- 1 teaspoon baking soda
- 1/2 teaspoon salt
- 1 teaspoon ground cinnamon
- 4 large eggs
- 1/2 cup unsweetened applesauce
- 1/4 cup coconut oil, melted
- 1/4 cup almond milk or any milk of your choice
- 1/4 cup sugar substitute (like stevia or erythritol)
- 1 teaspoon vanilla extract
- 1 cup diced apples (peeled and cored)

Instructions:

Preheat your oven to 350°F (175°C). Line a muffin tin with paper liners or grease each cup.

In a large bowl, whisk together almond flour, coconut flour, baking soda, salt, and ground cinnamon.

In a separate bowl, beat the eggs. Add applesauce, melted coconut oil, almond milk, sugar substitute, and vanilla extract. Mix until well combined.

Pour the wet ingredients into the dry ingredients and stir until just combined.

Fold in the diced apples until evenly distributed throughout the batter.

Spoon the batter into the prepared muffin cups, filling each about 2/3 full.

Bake in the preheated oven for 20-25 minutes or until a toothpick inserted into the center comes out clean.

Allow the muffins to cool in the tin for 5 minutes before transferring them to a wire rack to cool completely.

Enjoy these Sugar-Free Apple Cinnamon Muffins as a delicious and guilt-free treat!

Raspberry Almond Thumbprint Cookies

Ingredients:

- 1 cup almond flour
- 1/4 cup coconut flour
- 1/4 cup coconut oil, melted
- 3 tablespoons maple syrup or any sugar substitute
- 1/2 teaspoon almond extract
- 1/4 cup raspberry jam (sugar-free if preferred)
- Sliced almonds for topping

Instructions:

Preheat your oven to 350°F (175°C). Line a baking sheet with parchment paper.
In a bowl, combine almond flour, coconut flour, melted coconut oil, maple syrup (or sugar substitute), and almond extract. Mix until a dough forms.
Take small portions of the dough and roll them into balls.
Place the balls on the prepared baking sheet, spacing them apart.
Use your thumb or the back of a spoon to make an indentation in the center of each cookie.
Fill each indentation with a small amount of raspberry jam.
Top each cookie with sliced almonds.
Bake in the preheated oven for 10-12 minutes or until the edges are golden brown.
Allow the Raspberry Almond Thumbprint Cookies to cool on the baking sheet for a few minutes before transferring them to a wire rack to cool completely.
Once cooled, store in an airtight container and enjoy these delightful and gluten-free cookies!

Chocolate Avocado Truffles

Ingredients:

- 2 ripe avocados
- 1/2 cup unsweetened cocoa powder
- 1/4 cup maple syrup or any sweetener of your choice
- 1 teaspoon vanilla extract
- Pinch of salt
- 1/2 cup dark chocolate chips (70% cocoa or higher)
- Optional coatings: cocoa powder, shredded coconut, chopped nuts

Instructions:

Cut the avocados in half, remove the pit, and scoop out the flesh.
In a blender or food processor, combine the avocado flesh, cocoa powder, maple syrup, vanilla extract, and a pinch of salt.
Blend the ingredients until smooth and creamy, scraping down the sides of the blender or food processor as needed.
In a microwave-safe bowl or using a double boiler, melt the dark chocolate chips.
Add the melted chocolate to the avocado mixture and blend until well combined.
Place the truffle mixture in the refrigerator for about 1-2 hours to firm up.
Once chilled, scoop out small portions of the mixture and roll them into bite-sized truffles using your hands.
Roll the truffles in cocoa powder, shredded coconut, chopped nuts, or any preferred coating.
Place the Chocolate Avocado Truffles on a parchment-lined tray or plate.
Refrigerate the truffles for at least 30 minutes to allow them to set.
Once set, transfer the truffles to an airtight container for storage.
Enjoy these rich and creamy Chocolate Avocado Truffles as a healthier alternative to traditional chocolate truffles!

Vanilla Chia Pudding with Fresh Berries

Ingredients:

- 1/4 cup chia seeds
- 1 cup almond milk or any milk of your choice
- 1 tablespoon maple syrup or any sweetener of your choice
- 1 teaspoon vanilla extract
- Mixed fresh berries (strawberries, blueberries, raspberries) for topping
- Optional toppings: sliced almonds, shredded coconut

Instructions:

In a bowl, whisk together chia seeds, almond milk, maple syrup, and vanilla extract.

Whisk the mixture well to ensure the chia seeds are evenly distributed.

Cover the bowl and refrigerate the chia pudding for at least 2 hours or overnight, allowing it to thicken.

Before serving, give the chia pudding a good stir to ensure it has a smooth consistency.

Spoon the vanilla chia pudding into serving glasses or bowls.

Top the chia pudding with fresh mixed berries.

Optional: Add additional toppings such as sliced almonds or shredded coconut for extra texture.

Serve and enjoy this Vanilla Chia Pudding with Fresh Berries as a delicious and nutritious breakfast or snack!

Low-Sugar Mango Sorbet

Ingredients:

- 2 cups frozen mango chunks
- 1 tablespoon lime juice
- 2-3 tablespoons water
- 1-2 tablespoons honey or any sweetener of your choice (optional, depending on sweetness preference)

Instructions:

Place the frozen mango chunks in a blender or food processor.
Add lime juice and start blending the mango chunks.
Gradually add water, 1 tablespoon at a time, until the mixture reaches a smooth consistency. Be cautious not to add too much water, as you want a thick sorbet texture.
Taste the sorbet mixture and add honey or sweetener if desired. Blend again to combine.
Stop the blender and scrape down the sides if needed to ensure everything is well mixed.
Once the sorbet has a smooth and creamy consistency, transfer it to a shallow dish or pan.
Smooth the top with a spatula or spoon.
Place the dish in the freezer for at least 2-3 hours or until the sorbet is firm.
Before serving, let the sorbet sit at room temperature for a few minutes to soften slightly.
Scoop the Low-Sugar Mango Sorbet into bowls or cones.
Enjoy this refreshing and naturally sweet treat with significantly less sugar than traditional sorbets!

Pumpkin Spice Energy Bites

Ingredients:

- 1 cup old-fashioned oats
- 1/2 cup pumpkin puree
- 1/4 cup almond butter or any nut/seed butter
- 1/4 cup honey or maple syrup
- 1 teaspoon pumpkin spice blend (or a mixture of cinnamon, nutmeg, and cloves)
- 1/2 teaspoon vanilla extract
- Pinch of salt
- 1/3 cup mini chocolate chips (optional, or use chopped nuts or dried fruit)

Instructions:

In a large mixing bowl, combine oats, pumpkin puree, almond butter, honey or maple syrup, pumpkin spice blend, vanilla extract, and a pinch of salt.
Mix the ingredients until well combined.
If using, fold in mini chocolate chips or other add-ins of your choice.
Place the mixture in the refrigerator for about 15-30 minutes to firm up slightly.
After chilling, take small portions of the mixture and roll them into bite-sized energy bites using your hands.
Place the Pumpkin Spice Energy Bites on a parchment-lined tray or plate.
Refrigerate the energy bites for at least 30 minutes to allow them to set.
Once set, transfer the energy bites to an airtight container for storage.
Enjoy these Pumpkin Spice Energy Bites as a delicious and nutritious snack, perfect for a boost of energy during the day!

Cinnamon Baked Apples

Ingredients:

- 4 medium-sized apples (such as Granny Smith or Honeycrisp)
- 2 tablespoons melted coconut oil or unsalted butter
- 2 tablespoons honey or maple syrup
- 1 teaspoon ground cinnamon
- 1/4 teaspoon ground nutmeg
- 1/4 teaspoon vanilla extract
- Pinch of salt
- Chopped nuts or granola for topping (optional)
- Greek yogurt or vanilla ice cream for serving (optional)

Instructions:

Preheat your oven to 375°F (190°C).
Wash and core the apples, leaving the bottoms intact.
In a small bowl, mix together melted coconut oil or butter, honey or maple syrup, ground cinnamon, ground nutmeg, vanilla extract, and a pinch of salt.
Place the cored apples in a baking dish.
Brush the inside and tops of the apples with the cinnamon mixture, ensuring they are well coated.
If desired, fill the centers of the apples with chopped nuts or granola.
Bake in the preheated oven for 25-30 minutes or until the apples are tender.
Remove the baked apples from the oven and let them cool for a few minutes.
Serve the Cinnamon Baked Apples warm, either on their own or with a dollop of Greek yogurt or a scoop of vanilla ice cream.
Enjoy this simple and comforting dessert that highlights the natural sweetness of apples!

Sugar-Free Chocolate Pudding

Ingredients:

- 2 ripe avocados
- 1/2 cup unsweetened cocoa powder
- 1/4 cup almond milk or any milk of your choice
- 1/4 cup sugar substitute (like stevia or erythritol)
- 1 teaspoon vanilla extract
- Pinch of salt

Instructions:

Cut the avocados in half, remove the pit, and scoop out the flesh.
In a blender or food processor, combine the avocado flesh, cocoa powder, almond milk, sugar substitute, vanilla extract, and a pinch of salt.
Blend the ingredients until smooth and creamy, scraping down the sides of the blender or food processor as needed.
Taste the chocolate pudding mixture and adjust the sweetness if necessary by adding more sugar substitute.
Once the Sugar-Free Chocolate Pudding is smooth and well-blended, transfer it to serving bowls or glasses.
Refrigerate the pudding for at least 1-2 hours to chill and set.
Before serving, you can garnish the pudding with a sprinkle of cocoa powder or a few berries.
Enjoy this creamy and sugar-free chocolate treat as a guilt-free dessert or snack!

Almond Joy Protein Bars

Ingredients:

- 1 cup almond butter
- 1/4 cup coconut flour
- 1/4 cup unsweetened shredded coconut
- 1/4 cup chocolate protein powder
- 2 tablespoons maple syrup or any sweetener of your choice
- 1/2 teaspoon almond extract
- 1/4 cup dark chocolate chips (70% cocoa or higher)
- Additional shredded coconut for topping (optional)

Instructions:

In a mixing bowl, combine almond butter, coconut flour, shredded coconut, chocolate protein powder, maple syrup, and almond extract.
Mix the ingredients until a thick, dough-like consistency forms.
Fold in the dark chocolate chips.
Line a square baking dish with parchment paper, leaving some overhang for easy removal.
Press the almond joy mixture evenly into the bottom of the dish.
If desired, sprinkle additional shredded coconut on top and press it into the mixture.
Place the dish in the refrigerator for at least 2 hours to allow the bars to set.
Once set, lift the almond joy mixture out of the dish using the parchment paper overhang.
Cut into bars or squares.
Store the Almond Joy Protein Bars in an airtight container in the refrigerator.
Enjoy these delicious and protein-packed bars as a healthy snack or post-workout treat!

Keto Cheesecake Bites

Ingredients:

For the crust:

- 1 cup almond flour
- 2 tablespoons coconut flour
- 2 tablespoons melted butter
- 1 tablespoon powdered erythritol or any keto-friendly sweetener
- 1/2 teaspoon vanilla extract
- Pinch of salt

For the filling:

- 8 ounces cream cheese, softened
- 1/3 cup powdered erythritol or any keto-friendly sweetener
- 1 teaspoon vanilla extract
- 1/2 teaspoon lemon juice (optional)
- 2 large eggs

Instructions:

Preheat your oven to 325°F (163°C). Line a mini muffin tin with paper liners.
In a bowl, combine almond flour, coconut flour, melted butter, powdered erythritol, vanilla extract, and a pinch of salt for the crust. Mix until well combined.
Press a small amount of the crust mixture into the bottom of each mini muffin cup to form the crust.
In a separate bowl, beat the softened cream cheese until smooth.
Add powdered erythritol, vanilla extract, and lemon juice (if using) to the cream cheese. Mix until well combined.
Add the eggs to the cream cheese mixture, one at a time, beating well after each addition.
Spoon the cream cheese filling over the crust in each muffin cup, filling almost to the top.
Bake in the preheated oven for about 15-20 minutes or until the cheesecake bites are set and slightly golden around the edges.

Allow the Keto Cheesecake Bites to cool in the muffin tin for 10-15 minutes before transferring them to a wire rack to cool completely.
Refrigerate the cheesecake bites for at least 2 hours or overnight before serving.
Serve chilled and enjoy these delicious Keto Cheesecake Bites as a low-carb and satisfying dessert!

Blueberry Coconut Milk Ice Cream

Ingredients:

- 2 cups fresh or frozen blueberries
- 1 can (14 ounces) coconut milk (full-fat)
- 1/2 cup unsweetened shredded coconut
- 1/3 cup honey or any sweetener of your choice
- 1 teaspoon vanilla extract
- Pinch of salt

Instructions:

In a blender, combine blueberries, coconut milk, shredded coconut, honey, vanilla extract, and a pinch of salt.
Blend the ingredients until smooth and well combined.
Taste the mixture and adjust the sweetness if necessary by adding more honey.
Pour the blueberry coconut mixture into an ice cream maker.
Churn the mixture in the ice cream maker according to the manufacturer's instructions until it reaches a soft-serve consistency.
If you don't have an ice cream maker, you can pour the mixture into a shallow dish and freeze it. Every 30 minutes, stir the mixture with a fork to break up ice crystals until it reaches the desired consistency.
Transfer the churned or frozen ice cream to a lidded container and freeze for an additional 2-4 hours to firm up.
Before serving, let the Blueberry Coconut Milk Ice Cream sit at room temperature for a few minutes to soften slightly.
Scoop and enjoy this refreshing and dairy-free Blueberry Coconut Milk Ice Cream!

No-Bake Almond Butter Cups

Ingredients:

For the filling:

- 1/2 cup almond butter
- 2 tablespoons coconut flour
- 2 tablespoons melted coconut oil
- 1 tablespoon maple syrup or any sweetener of your choice
- 1/2 teaspoon vanilla extract
- Pinch of salt

For the chocolate coating:

- 1/2 cup dark chocolate chips (70% cocoa or higher)
- 1 tablespoon coconut oil

Instructions:

In a bowl, mix together almond butter, coconut flour, melted coconut oil, maple syrup, vanilla extract, and a pinch of salt until well combined.
In a separate bowl, melt the dark chocolate chips and coconut oil together. You can do this in a microwave or using a double boiler.
Line a mini muffin tin with paper liners.
Spoon a small amount of the melted chocolate into the bottom of each cup, spreading it to cover the bottom.
Place the muffin tin in the freezer for a few minutes to allow the chocolate to set.
Once the chocolate is firm, spoon a small portion of the almond butter filling into each cup, pressing it down gently.
Pour the remaining melted chocolate over the almond butter filling, covering it completely.
Place the muffin tin back in the freezer and let the almond butter cups set for at least 2 hours.
Once set, remove the almond butter cups from the freezer and let them sit at room temperature for a few minutes before serving.
Enjoy these delicious No-Bake Almond Butter Cups as a satisfying and healthier alternative to traditional peanut butter cups!

Vanilla Ricotta Stuffed Strawberries

Ingredients:

- 1 cup ricotta cheese
- 1 tablespoon honey or maple syrup
- 1 teaspoon vanilla extract
- Zest of one lemon (optional)
- Fresh strawberries, washed and hulled
- Mint leaves for garnish (optional)

Instructions:

In a bowl, mix together ricotta cheese, honey or maple syrup, vanilla extract, and lemon zest (if using). Stir until well combined.

Use a small spoon or a piping bag to fill each strawberry with the vanilla ricotta mixture.

Garnish with mint leaves, if desired.

Serve the Vanilla Ricotta Stuffed Strawberries immediately or refrigerate until ready to serve.

Enjoy these elegant and flavorful stuffed strawberries as a light and refreshing dessert or snack!

Sugar-Free Lemon Bars

Ingredients:

For the crust:

- 1 cup almond flour
- 1/4 cup coconut flour
- 1/4 cup melted butter or coconut oil
- 2 tablespoons powdered erythritol or any sugar substitute
- Pinch of salt

For the filling:

- 4 large eggs
- 1 cup powdered erythritol or any sugar substitute
- 1/2 cup fresh lemon juice (about 4-5 lemons)
- Zest of 2 lemons
- 1/4 cup almond flour
- 1/2 teaspoon baking powder
- Powdered erythritol for dusting (optional)

Instructions:

Preheat your oven to 350°F (175°C). Line an 8x8-inch baking pan with parchment paper, leaving some overhang for easy removal.
In a bowl, combine almond flour, coconut flour, melted butter or coconut oil, powdered erythritol, and a pinch of salt for the crust. Mix until well combined.
Press the crust mixture into the bottom of the prepared baking pan.
Bake the crust in the preheated oven for 10-12 minutes or until it starts to turn golden brown.
While the crust is baking, prepare the filling. In a mixing bowl, whisk together eggs, powdered erythritol, lemon juice, lemon zest, almond flour, and baking powder until smooth.
Pour the filling over the partially baked crust.
Bake in the oven for an additional 20-25 minutes or until the filling is set and the edges are golden brown.

Allow the Sugar-Free Lemon Bars to cool in the pan for at least 1 hour.
Once cooled, refrigerate for an additional 2 hours or until fully chilled.
Use the parchment paper overhang to lift the bars out of the pan.
Optional: Dust the top of the bars with powdered erythritol before slicing into squares.
Serve and enjoy these delicious Sugar-Free Lemon Bars as a guilt-free treat!

Chocolate Covered Almonds

Ingredients:

- 1 cup whole almonds
- 1/2 cup dark chocolate chips (70% cocoa or higher)
- 1 tablespoon coconut oil
- 1/2 teaspoon vanilla extract
- Pinch of salt
- Optional: Unsweetened shredded coconut, sea salt, or cocoa powder for coating

Instructions:

Line a baking sheet with parchment paper.
In a heatproof bowl, combine the dark chocolate chips and coconut oil.
Melt the chocolate and coconut oil together using a double boiler or by microwaving in 20-second increments, stirring between each increment until smooth.
Stir in vanilla extract and a pinch of salt into the melted chocolate mixture.
Dip each almond into the chocolate mixture, ensuring it is well coated.
Use a fork or a chocolate dipper to lift the chocolate-covered almonds, allowing any excess chocolate to drip off.
Place the dipped almonds on the prepared baking sheet, ensuring they are not touching.
Optional: Sprinkle the chocolate-covered almonds with unsweetened shredded coconut, a pinch of sea salt, or dust them with cocoa powder.
Allow the chocolate-covered almonds to set at room temperature or refrigerate for faster setting.
Once the chocolate is fully set, transfer the chocolate-covered almonds to an airtight container.
Enjoy these homemade Chocolate Covered Almonds as a delicious and satisfying snack!

Blackberry Coconut Chia Seed Pudding

Ingredients:

- 1/2 cup chia seeds
- 2 cups coconut milk
- 1 teaspoon vanilla extract
- 2 tablespoons maple syrup or any sweetener of your choice
- 1 cup fresh blackberries
- Shredded coconut for garnish (optional)

Instructions:

In a bowl, whisk together chia seeds, coconut milk, vanilla extract, and maple syrup.
Stir the mixture well to ensure the chia seeds are evenly distributed.
Cover the bowl and refrigerate the chia seed pudding for at least 2 hours or overnight, allowing it to thicken.
Before serving, give the chia pudding a good stir to ensure it has a smooth consistency.
In a blender or food processor, blend fresh blackberries until smooth.
Layer the chia seed pudding and blackberry puree in serving glasses or bowls.
Optional: Garnish the Blackberry Coconut Chia Seed Pudding with shredded coconut for added texture.
Serve and enjoy this refreshing and nutrient-rich pudding as a breakfast, snack, or dessert!

Low-Sugar Oatmeal Cookies

Ingredients:

- 1 cup old-fashioned oats
- 1/2 cup almond flour
- 1/4 cup coconut flour
- 1/2 teaspoon baking powder
- 1/4 teaspoon baking soda
- 1/4 teaspoon salt
- 1/4 cup coconut oil, melted
- 1/4 cup unsweetened applesauce
- 1/4 cup maple syrup or any sugar substitute of your choice
- 1 teaspoon vanilla extract
- 1/4 cup chopped nuts (such as walnuts or almonds)
- 1/4 cup raisins or dried cranberries (optional)

Instructions:

Preheat your oven to 350°F (175°C). Line a baking sheet with parchment paper.
In a large bowl, combine old-fashioned oats, almond flour, coconut flour, baking powder, baking soda, and salt. Mix well.
In a separate bowl, whisk together melted coconut oil, applesauce, maple syrup, and vanilla extract.
Add the wet ingredients to the dry ingredients and mix until a dough forms.
Fold in chopped nuts and raisins or dried cranberries if using.
Drop spoonfuls of cookie dough onto the prepared baking sheet, spacing them apart.
Use the back of a spoon to flatten and shape each cookie.
Bake in the preheated oven for 10-12 minutes or until the edges are golden brown.
Allow the Low-Sugar Oatmeal Cookies to cool on the baking sheet for a few minutes before transferring them to a wire rack to cool completely.
Once cooled, store the cookies in an airtight container.
Enjoy these healthier oatmeal cookies with reduced sugar content as a tasty snack or treat!

Pistachio Dark Chocolate Bark

Ingredients:

- 1 cup dark chocolate chips (70% cocoa or higher)
- 1/2 cup shelled pistachios, roughly chopped
- 1/4 cup unsweetened shredded coconut
- Sea salt for sprinkling (optional)

Instructions:

Line a baking sheet with parchment paper.
In a heatproof bowl, melt the dark chocolate chips using a double boiler or by microwaving in 20-second increments, stirring between each increment until smooth.
Once the chocolate is fully melted, spread it evenly onto the prepared baking sheet.
Sprinkle the chopped pistachios and shredded coconut evenly over the melted chocolate.
If desired, lightly sprinkle sea salt over the top for a sweet and salty flavor.
Place the baking sheet in the refrigerator for at least 30 minutes or until the chocolate has completely set.
Once set, break the Pistachio Dark Chocolate Bark into bite-sized pieces.
Store in an airtight container in the refrigerator.
Enjoy this delicious and satisfying Pistachio Dark Chocolate Bark as a sweet treat or snack!

Peach and Raspberry Yogurt Popsicles

Ingredients:

- 1 cup fresh or frozen raspberries
- 2 ripe peaches, peeled and sliced
- 2 cups Greek yogurt
- 1/4 cup honey or maple syrup (adjust to taste)
- 1 teaspoon vanilla extract

Instructions:

In a blender or food processor, puree the raspberries until smooth. Strain the puree to remove seeds, if desired.
In the same blender, puree the sliced peaches until smooth.
In a bowl, mix Greek yogurt, honey or maple syrup, and vanilla extract until well combined.
In your popsicle molds, layer the yogurt mixture and fruit purees alternately. You can create a marbled effect by swirling the layers with a toothpick or skewer.
Insert popsicle sticks into the molds.
Freeze the Peach and Raspberry Yogurt Popsicles for at least 4-6 hours or until fully set.
Once frozen, run the molds under warm water for a few seconds to release the popsicles.
Enjoy these refreshing and fruity popsicles on a hot day!

Walnut and Date Energy Bites

Ingredients:

- 1 cup walnuts
- 1 cup pitted dates
- 1/4 cup shredded coconut (unsweetened)
- 1 tablespoon chia seeds
- 1 tablespoon flaxseeds
- 1 teaspoon vanilla extract
- Pinch of salt

Instructions:

In a food processor, combine walnuts, pitted dates, shredded coconut, chia seeds, flaxseeds, vanilla extract, and a pinch of salt.

Pulse the ingredients until they are finely chopped and the mixture starts to come together.

Check the consistency by pinching a small amount of the mixture between your fingers. If it holds together, it's ready; otherwise, pulse a bit more.

Scoop out tablespoon-sized portions of the mixture and roll them into balls using your hands.

Place the Walnut and Date Energy Bites on a plate or tray lined with parchment paper.

Refrigerate the energy bites for at least 30 minutes to firm up.

Once firm, transfer the energy bites to an airtight container and store in the refrigerator.

Enjoy these Walnut and Date Energy Bites as a quick and nutritious snack or energy boost!

Berry and Greek Yogurt Frozen Bites

Ingredients:

- 1 cup mixed berries (such as strawberries, blueberries, raspberries)
- 1 cup Greek yogurt
- 2 tablespoons honey or maple syrup (optional, depending on sweetness preference)

Instructions:

In a blender or food processor, puree the mixed berries until smooth.
In a bowl, mix the Greek yogurt with honey or maple syrup, if using.
Line a mini muffin tin with paper liners.
Spoon a small amount of the berry puree into each cup, filling it about one-third of the way.
Add a layer of Greek yogurt on top of the berry puree, filling the cups to about two-thirds full.
Repeat the process, alternating between berry puree and Greek yogurt until the cups are almost full.
Use a toothpick or skewer to swirl the layers together, creating a marbled effect.
Place the muffin tin in the freezer and let the Berry and Greek Yogurt Frozen Bites set for at least 4-6 hours or until fully frozen.
Once frozen, remove the bites from the muffin tin.
Allow them to sit at room temperature for a few minutes before serving.
Enjoy these refreshing and nutritious frozen bites as a cool treat!

Sugar-Free Lemon Sorbet

Ingredients:

- 1 cup water
- 1 cup fresh lemon juice (about 6-8 lemons)
- 1 tablespoon lemon zest
- 1/2 cup powdered erythritol or any sugar substitute
- 1/2 teaspoon vanilla extract (optional)

Instructions:

In a saucepan, combine water and powdered erythritol. Heat over medium heat, stirring until the erythritol dissolves. Allow the mixture to cool.

In a large bowl, mix the fresh lemon juice, lemon zest, and vanilla extract (if using) with the cooled erythritol syrup.

Pour the lemon mixture into an ice cream maker and churn according to the manufacturer's instructions until it reaches a sorbet consistency.

Transfer the sorbet to a lidded container and freeze for at least 2-4 hours to firm up.

Before serving, let the Sugar-Free Lemon Sorbet sit at room temperature for a few minutes to soften slightly.

Scoop and enjoy this refreshing and sugar-free lemon treat!

Note: If you don't have an ice cream maker, you can pour the mixture into a shallow dish and freeze it. Every 30 minutes, stir the mixture with a fork to break up ice crystals until it reaches the desired consistency.

Almond Flour Pumpkin Muffins

Ingredients:

- 2 cups almond flour
- 1/2 cup coconut flour
- 1 teaspoon baking powder
- 1/2 teaspoon baking soda
- 1/4 teaspoon salt
- 1 teaspoon ground cinnamon
- 1/2 teaspoon ground nutmeg
- 1/4 teaspoon ground cloves
- 1/4 cup melted coconut oil
- 1/2 cup pumpkin puree
- 1/3 cup maple syrup or any sweetener of your choice
- 3 large eggs
- 1 teaspoon vanilla extract
- 1/2 cup chopped walnuts or pecans (optional)

Instructions:

Preheat your oven to 350°F (175°C). Line a muffin tin with paper liners.
In a large bowl, whisk together almond flour, coconut flour, baking powder, baking soda, salt, cinnamon, nutmeg, and cloves.
In another bowl, mix melted coconut oil, pumpkin puree, maple syrup, eggs, and vanilla extract.
Pour the wet ingredients into the dry ingredients and stir until well combined.
If using, fold in chopped nuts.
Spoon the batter into the prepared muffin tin, filling each cup about 2/3 full.
Bake in the preheated oven for 20-25 minutes or until a toothpick inserted into the center comes out clean.
Allow the Almond Flour Pumpkin Muffins to cool in the muffin tin for 5 minutes before transferring them to a wire rack to cool completely.
Enjoy these delicious and gluten-free pumpkin muffins as a wholesome breakfast or snack!

Raspberry Coconut Chia Jam

Ingredients:

- 2 cups fresh or frozen raspberries
- 2 tablespoons chia seeds
- 2 tablespoons maple syrup or any sweetener of your choice
- 1 teaspoon vanilla extract (optional)
- 1-2 tablespoons shredded coconut (optional)

Instructions:

In a saucepan, heat the raspberries over medium heat until they start to break down and release their juices.
Use a potato masher or fork to mash the raspberries to your desired consistency.
Stir in the chia seeds and continue to cook over medium heat, stirring frequently.
Add maple syrup and vanilla extract (if using), adjusting the sweetness to your liking.
Continue to cook the mixture until it thickens to a jam-like consistency, which typically takes about 10-15 minutes.
Remove the saucepan from heat and let the Raspberry Coconut Chia Jam cool for a few minutes.
If desired, stir in shredded coconut for added texture.
Transfer the jam to a jar or airtight container and refrigerate for at least 1-2 hours to allow it to set.
Use the jam as a topping for toast, pancakes, yogurt, or as a filling for pastries.
Enjoy the homemade Raspberry Coconut Chia Jam as a delicious and healthier alternative to store-bought jams!

Chocolate Avocado Popsicles

Ingredients:

- 2 ripe avocados, peeled and pitted
- 1/2 cup cocoa powder
- 1/2 cup coconut milk
- 1/3 cup maple syrup or any sweetener of your choice
- 1 teaspoon vanilla extract
- Pinch of salt

Instructions:

In a blender or food processor, combine ripe avocados, cocoa powder, coconut milk, maple syrup, vanilla extract, and a pinch of salt.
Blend the ingredients until smooth and well combined.
Taste the mixture and adjust the sweetness if necessary by adding more maple syrup.
Pour the chocolate avocado mixture into popsicle molds.
Insert popsicle sticks into the molds.
Place the molds in the freezer and let the Chocolate Avocado Popsicles set for at least 4-6 hours or until fully frozen.
Once frozen, run the molds under warm water for a few seconds to release the popsicles.
Enjoy these creamy and chocolatey popsicles as a refreshing and guilt-free treat!

No-Bake Coconut Cashew Bars

Ingredients:

For the base:

- 1 cup pitted dates
- 1 cup unsalted cashews
- 1/2 cup shredded coconut (unsweetened)
- 2 tablespoons coconut oil, melted
- Pinch of salt

For the topping:

- 1/2 cup shredded coconut (unsweetened)
- 1/4 cup cashews, chopped

Instructions:

Line a square baking dish with parchment paper, leaving some overhang for easy removal.
In a food processor, combine pitted dates, unsalted cashews, shredded coconut, melted coconut oil, and a pinch of salt.
Process the ingredients until they form a sticky and crumbly mixture.
Press the mixture firmly into the bottom of the prepared baking dish to form an even layer.
For the topping, sprinkle shredded coconut and chopped cashews over the base layer, pressing them gently into the mixture.
Place the baking dish in the refrigerator and let the No-Bake Coconut Cashew Bars set for at least 2 hours.
Once set, use the parchment paper overhang to lift the bars out of the dish.
Cut into squares or bars.
Store the bars in an airtight container in the refrigerator.
Enjoy these delicious and wholesome No-Bake Coconut Cashew Bars as a snack or dessert!

Low-Sugar Blueberry Cheesecake

Ingredients:

For the crust:

- 1 cup almond flour
- 1/4 cup melted coconut oil
- 1 tablespoon powdered erythritol or any sugar substitute
- Pinch of salt

For the filling:

- 2 cups cream cheese, softened
- 1/2 cup powdered erythritol or any sugar substitute
- 2 large eggs
- 1 teaspoon vanilla extract

For the blueberry topping:

- 1 cup fresh or frozen blueberries
- 2 tablespoons water
- 1 tablespoon powdered erythritol or any sugar substitute
- 1 teaspoon lemon juice

Instructions:

Preheat your oven to 325°F (163°C). Grease a round cake pan or springform pan.
In a bowl, combine almond flour, melted coconut oil, powdered erythritol, and a pinch of salt for the crust. Mix until well combined.
Press the crust mixture into the bottom of the prepared pan, creating an even layer.
In a separate bowl, beat together softened cream cheese, powdered erythritol, eggs, and vanilla extract until smooth and creamy.
Pour the cream cheese mixture over the crust in the pan, spreading it evenly.
Bake in the preheated oven for 25-30 minutes or until the edges are set, and the center is slightly jiggly.

Allow the cheesecake to cool to room temperature and then refrigerate for at least 4 hours or overnight to set.

For the blueberry topping, in a saucepan, combine blueberries, water, powdered erythritol, and lemon juice. Simmer over medium heat until the blueberries break down and the mixture thickens.

Let the blueberry topping cool before spreading it over the chilled cheesecake. Once the topping is set, slice and serve the Low-Sugar Blueberry Cheesecake. Enjoy this delicious and lower-sugar alternative to traditional cheesecake!

Cacao Nib and Coconut Energy Bites

Ingredients:

- 1 cup rolled oats
- 1/2 cup almond butter
- 1/3 cup honey or maple syrup
- 1/4 cup cacao nibs
- 1/4 cup shredded coconut (unsweetened)
- 1 teaspoon vanilla extract
- Pinch of salt

Instructions:

In a food processor, combine rolled oats, almond butter, honey or maple syrup, cacao nibs, shredded coconut, vanilla extract, and a pinch of salt.
Process the ingredients until a sticky and well-combined mixture forms.
Scoop out tablespoon-sized portions of the mixture and roll them into balls using your hands.
Place the Cacao Nib and Coconut Energy Bites on a plate or tray lined with parchment paper.
Refrigerate the energy bites for at least 30 minutes to firm up.
Once firm, transfer the energy bites to an airtight container and store in the refrigerator.
Enjoy these delicious and nutrient-packed energy bites as a quick and wholesome snack!

Lemon Poppy Seed Ricotta Cake

Ingredients:

For the Cake:

- 1 1/2 cups all-purpose flour
- 1 1/2 teaspoons baking powder
- 1/4 teaspoon salt
- 1 cup ricotta cheese
- 1 cup granulated sugar
- 3 large eggs
- 1/2 cup unsalted butter, melted
- Zest of 2 lemons
- 2 tablespoons lemon juice
- 1 teaspoon vanilla extract
- 1 tablespoon poppy seeds

For the Glaze:

- 1 cup powdered sugar
- 2 tablespoons lemon juice
- Zest of 1 lemon

Instructions:

Preheat your oven to 350°F (175°C). Grease and flour a 9-inch round cake pan.
In a bowl, whisk together the flour, baking powder, and salt. Set aside.
In a separate large bowl, combine ricotta cheese, granulated sugar, and eggs. Mix until smooth.
Add melted butter, lemon zest, lemon juice, and vanilla extract to the ricotta mixture. Mix until well combined.
Gradually add the dry ingredients to the wet ingredients, mixing until just combined.
Fold in the poppy seeds.
Pour the batter into the prepared cake pan and smooth the top with a spatula.

Bake in the preheated oven for 35-40 minutes or until a toothpick inserted into the center comes out clean.

Allow the cake to cool in the pan for 10 minutes before transferring it to a wire rack to cool completely.

For the glaze, whisk together powdered sugar, lemon juice, and lemon zest until smooth.

Drizzle the glaze over the cooled Lemon Poppy Seed Ricotta Cake.

Slice and serve this delicious and moist cake with a delightful lemon flavor!

Vanilla Almond Protein Bites

Ingredients:

- 1 cup rolled oats
- 1/2 cup vanilla protein powder
- 1/2 cup almond butter
- 1/4 cup honey or maple syrup
- 1 teaspoon vanilla extract
- 1/4 cup chopped almonds
- Pinch of salt

Instructions:

In a food processor, combine rolled oats, vanilla protein powder, almond butter, honey or maple syrup, vanilla extract, and a pinch of salt.
Process the ingredients until a sticky and well-combined mixture forms.
Transfer the mixture to a bowl and fold in the chopped almonds.
Scoop out tablespoon-sized portions of the mixture and roll them into balls using your hands.
Place the Vanilla Almond Protein Bites on a plate or tray lined with parchment paper.
Refrigerate the protein bites for at least 30 minutes to firm up.
Once firm, transfer the protein bites to an airtight container and store in the refrigerator.
Enjoy these nutritious and protein-packed bites as a convenient snack or energy boost!

Sugar-Free Apple Pie Bites

Ingredients:

For the Filling:

- 2 cups finely diced apples (peeled and cored)
- 1 teaspoon ground cinnamon
- 1/4 teaspoon ground nutmeg

- 1 tablespoon lemon juice
- 2 tablespoons powdered erythritol or any sugar substitute
- 1 tablespoon water

For the Dough:

- 1 cup almond flour
- 2 tablespoons coconut flour
- 1/4 cup melted coconut oil
- 2 tablespoons powdered erythritol or any sugar substitute
- 1 teaspoon vanilla extract
- Pinch of salt

Instructions:

Preheat your oven to 350°F (175°C). Line a baking sheet with parchment paper.
In a saucepan, combine finely diced apples, ground cinnamon, ground nutmeg, lemon juice, powdered erythritol, and water. Cook over medium heat for 5-7 minutes or until the apples are soft. Set aside to cool.
In a bowl, mix almond flour, coconut flour, melted coconut oil, powdered erythritol, vanilla extract, and a pinch of salt. Stir until a dough forms.
Divide the dough into equal portions and roll each portion into a ball.
Place a ball of dough on a sheet of parchment paper and use another sheet on top to roll out the dough into a thin circle.
Spoon a small amount of the cooled apple filling onto the center of the dough circle.
Carefully fold the edges of the dough up and over the filling, creating a small, sealed pie bite.
Repeat the process with the remaining dough and filling.
Place the Sugar-Free Apple Pie Bites on the prepared baking sheet.
Bake in the preheated oven for 12-15 minutes or until the edges are golden brown.
Allow the bites to cool before serving.
Enjoy these delightful and sugar-free apple pie bites as a healthier alternative to traditional apple pie!

Cocoa Dusted Almonds

Ingredients:

- 2 cups whole almonds
- 1 tablespoon unsweetened cocoa powder
- 2 tablespoons powdered erythritol or any sugar substitute
- 1/2 teaspoon vanilla extract
- Pinch of salt

Instructions:

Preheat your oven to 325°F (163°C). Line a baking sheet with parchment paper.
In a bowl, combine whole almonds, cocoa powder, powdered erythritol, vanilla extract, and a pinch of salt. Stir until the almonds are well coated.
Spread the cocoa-dusted almonds in a single layer on the prepared baking sheet.
Bake in the preheated oven for 15-20 minutes, stirring halfway through, until the almonds are toasted and fragrant.
Remove the almonds from the oven and let them cool completely on the baking sheet.
Once cooled, transfer the Cocoa Dusted Almonds to an airtight container for storage.
Enjoy these cocoa-flavored almonds as a delicious and satisfying snack!

Keto Pumpkin Pie Fat Bombs

Ingredients:

For the Pumpkin Pie Filling:

- 1/2 cup canned pumpkin puree
- 2 tablespoons coconut oil, melted
- 2 tablespoons powdered erythritol or any keto-friendly sweetener
- 1/2 teaspoon pumpkin pie spice
- 1/2 teaspoon vanilla extract

For the Fat Bomb Coating:

- 1/4 cup unsweetened shredded coconut
- 1/2 teaspoon ground cinnamon

Instructions:

In a bowl, combine canned pumpkin puree, melted coconut oil, powdered erythritol, pumpkin pie spice, and vanilla extract. Mix until smooth and well combined.

Place the bowl in the refrigerator for about 15-20 minutes to firm up the mixture slightly.

Once the pumpkin pie filling is firmer, use your hands to roll small portions of the mixture into balls.

In a separate shallow dish, combine unsweetened shredded coconut and ground cinnamon.

Roll each pumpkin pie fat bomb in the coconut-cinnamon mixture until coated.

Place the coated fat bombs on a plate or tray lined with parchment paper.

Refrigerate the Keto Pumpkin Pie Fat Bombs for at least 1-2 hours or until they are firm.

Once firm, transfer the fat bombs to an airtight container and store in the refrigerator.

Enjoy these delicious and keto-friendly pumpkin pie fat bombs as a satisfying treat!

Hazelnut Chocolate Protein Balls

Ingredients:

- 1 cup hazelnuts
- 1 cup pitted dates
- 2 tablespoons cocoa powder
- 1 scoop chocolate protein powder
- 1 tablespoon almond butter
- 1 teaspoon vanilla extract
- Pinch of salt
- Water (as needed)

Instructions:

In a food processor, blend hazelnuts until finely ground.
Add pitted dates, cocoa powder, chocolate protein powder, almond butter, vanilla extract, and a pinch of salt to the ground hazelnuts in the food processor.
Process the mixture until it forms a sticky dough. If the mixture is too dry, add water, one tablespoon at a time, until the desired consistency is reached.
Scoop out tablespoon-sized portions of the mixture and roll them into balls using your hands.
Place the Hazelnut Chocolate Protein Balls on a plate or tray lined with parchment paper.
Refrigerate the protein balls for at least 30 minutes to firm up.
Once firm, transfer the protein balls to an airtight container and store in the refrigerator.
Enjoy these delicious and protein-packed hazelnut chocolate protein balls as a quick and nutritious snack!

Strawberry Coconut Milk Panna Cotta

Ingredients:

- 1 cup full-fat coconut milk
- 1 cup fresh strawberries, hulled and halved
- 1/4 cup honey or maple syrup
- 1 teaspoon vanilla extract
- 2 teaspoons gelatin
- 2 tablespoons water
- Fresh strawberries for garnish (optional)
- Shredded coconut for garnish (optional)

Instructions:

In a small bowl, combine gelatin and water. Allow it to sit for 5 minutes to bloom.
In a blender, combine coconut milk, fresh strawberries, honey or maple syrup, and vanilla extract. Blend until smooth.
Transfer the blended mixture to a saucepan and heat over medium heat until it just begins to simmer. Do not boil.
Remove the saucepan from heat and stir in the bloomed gelatin until fully dissolved.
Strain the mixture through a fine-mesh sieve to remove strawberry seeds.
Pour the strained mixture into serving glasses or molds.
Refrigerate the Strawberry Coconut Milk Panna Cotta for at least 4 hours or until set.
Once set, garnish with fresh strawberries and shredded coconut if desired.
Serve and enjoy this refreshing and dairy-free dessert!

Low-Sugar Carrot Cake Bites

Ingredients:

For the Carrot Cake Bites:

- 1 cup shredded carrots
- 1 cup almond flour
- 1/4 cup coconut flour
- 1/4 cup chopped walnuts or pecans
- 1/4 cup raisins or dried cranberries (unsweetened)
- 2 tablespoons powdered erythritol or any sugar substitute
- 1 teaspoon ground cinnamon
- 1/2 teaspoon ground ginger
- 1/4 teaspoon ground nutmeg
- Pinch of salt
- 2 tablespoons coconut oil, melted
- 1 teaspoon vanilla extract

For the Cream Cheese Frosting:

- 4 oz cream cheese, softened
- 2 tablespoons powdered erythritol or any sugar substitute
- 1/2 teaspoon vanilla extract

Instructions:

In a large bowl, combine shredded carrots, almond flour, coconut flour, chopped nuts, raisins or dried cranberries, powdered erythritol, ground cinnamon, ground ginger, ground nutmeg, and a pinch of salt.
Add melted coconut oil and vanilla extract to the dry mixture. Stir until well combined.
Form the mixture into bite-sized balls and place them on a parchment-lined tray.
In a separate bowl, beat together softened cream cheese, powdered erythritol, and vanilla extract until smooth.
Place the cream cheese frosting in a piping bag or a plastic sandwich bag with a corner snipped off.

Pipe a small amount of cream cheese frosting onto each Carrot Cake Bite. Refrigerate the Low-Sugar Carrot Cake Bites for at least 30 minutes to firm up. Once firm, transfer the bites to an airtight container and store in the refrigerator. Enjoy these delicious and low-sugar carrot cake bites as a guilt-free dessert or snack!

Mint Chocolate Avocado Ice Cream

Ingredients:

- 2 ripe avocados, peeled and pitted
- 1/2 cup unsweetened cocoa powder
- 1/2 cup coconut milk
- 1/3 cup honey or maple syrup
- 1 teaspoon peppermint extract
- 1/2 teaspoon vanilla extract
- Pinch of salt
- 1/4 cup dark chocolate chips or chunks

Instructions:

In a blender or food processor, combine ripe avocados, cocoa powder, coconut milk, honey or maple syrup, peppermint extract, vanilla extract, and a pinch of salt.
Blend the ingredients until smooth and well combined.
Taste the mixture and adjust the sweetness if necessary by adding more honey or maple syrup.
Stir in dark chocolate chips or chunks.
Pour the mint chocolate avocado mixture into an ice cream maker and churn according to the manufacturer's instructions until it reaches an ice cream consistency.
If you don't have an ice cream maker, you can pour the mixture into a shallow dish and freeze it. Every 30 minutes, stir the mixture with a fork to break up ice crystals until it reaches the desired consistency.
Transfer the Mint Chocolate Avocado Ice Cream to a lidded container and freeze for at least 2-4 hours to firm up.
Before serving, let the ice cream sit at room temperature for a few minutes to soften slightly.
Scoop and enjoy this refreshing and creamy mint chocolate treat!

Sugar-Free Cherry Almond Granola Bars

Ingredients:

- 1 1/2 cups rolled oats
- 1/2 cup almond flour
- 1/2 cup chopped almonds
- 1/4 cup unsweetened shredded coconut
- 1/4 cup dried cherries, chopped
- 1/4 cup powdered erythritol or any sugar substitute
- 1/4 cup almond butter
- 1/4 cup coconut oil, melted
- 1 teaspoon almond extract
- Pinch of salt

Instructions:

Preheat your oven to 350°F (175°C). Line a baking dish with parchment paper, leaving some overhang for easy removal.
In a large bowl, combine rolled oats, almond flour, chopped almonds, shredded coconut, dried cherries, powdered erythritol, and a pinch of salt.
In a small saucepan, heat almond butter and melted coconut oil over low heat until melted and well combined.
Remove the saucepan from heat and stir in almond extract.
Pour the wet ingredients over the dry ingredients in the bowl. Mix until everything is evenly coated.
Transfer the mixture to the prepared baking dish and press it down firmly to create an even layer.
Bake in the preheated oven for 15-20 minutes or until the edges are golden brown.
Allow the granola bars to cool completely in the baking dish before cutting them into bars.
Once cooled and cut, store the Sugar-Free Cherry Almond Granola Bars in an airtight container at room temperature or in the refrigerator.
Enjoy these delicious and sugar-free granola bars as a wholesome snack!

Coconut Lime Chia Seed Pudding

Ingredients:

- 1/4 cup chia seeds
- 1 cup coconut milk (canned, full-fat)
- 1/2 cup unsweetened almond milk
- 2 tablespoons maple syrup or sweetener of choice
- Zest of 1 lime
- 2 tablespoons fresh lime juice
- 1/2 teaspoon vanilla extract
- Shredded coconut and lime slices for garnish (optional)

Instructions:

In a bowl, whisk together chia seeds, coconut milk, almond milk, maple syrup, lime zest, lime juice, and vanilla extract.

Whisk the mixture thoroughly to ensure the chia seeds are well distributed.

Let the mixture sit for about 5 minutes, then whisk again to prevent clumping.

Cover the bowl and refrigerate the Coconut Lime Chia Seed Pudding for at least 4 hours or overnight. Stir the pudding occasionally during the first hour to prevent clumping.

Once the pudding has thickened to your liking, give it a final stir.

Serve the Coconut Lime Chia Seed Pudding in individual bowls or jars.

Garnish with shredded coconut and lime slices if desired.

Enjoy this refreshing and tropical chia seed pudding as a healthy dessert or breakfast option!

Almond Flour Chocolate Zucchini Bread

Ingredients:

- 1 1/2 cups almond flour
- 1/4 cup cocoa powder
- 1 teaspoon baking soda
- 1/4 teaspoon salt
- 1/2 teaspoon ground cinnamon
- 3 large eggs
- 1/4 cup coconut oil, melted
- 1/4 cup maple syrup or sweetener of choice
- 1 teaspoon vanilla extract
- 1 1/2 cups grated zucchini (about 1 medium-sized zucchini)
- 1/2 cup dark chocolate chips (optional)

Instructions:

Preheat your oven to 350°F (175°C). Grease a loaf pan and line it with parchment paper for easy removal.

In a large bowl, whisk together almond flour, cocoa powder, baking soda, salt, and ground cinnamon.

In another bowl, beat the eggs. Add melted coconut oil, maple syrup, and vanilla extract. Mix well.

Pour the wet ingredients into the dry ingredients and stir until just combined.

Fold in the grated zucchini and dark chocolate chips if using.

Pour the batter into the prepared loaf pan and spread it evenly.

Bake in the preheated oven for 45-55 minutes or until a toothpick inserted into the center comes out clean.

Allow the Almond Flour Chocolate Zucchini Bread to cool in the pan for 10 minutes, then transfer it to a wire rack to cool completely.

Once cooled, slice and enjoy this delicious and moist chocolate zucchini bread!

Vanilla Coconut Flour Cupcakes

Ingredients:

For the Cupcakes:

- 1/2 cup coconut flour
- 1/2 teaspoon baking powder
- 1/4 teaspoon salt
- 4 large eggs
- 1/2 cup coconut milk
- 1/4 cup coconut oil, melted
- 1/4 cup honey or sweetener of choice
- 1 teaspoon vanilla extract

For the Frosting:

- 1 cup coconut cream (chilled)
- 2 tablespoons honey or sweetener of choice
- 1 teaspoon vanilla extract

Instructions:

Preheat your oven to 350°F (175°C). Line a muffin tin with cupcake liners.
In a bowl, whisk together coconut flour, baking powder, and salt.
In another bowl, beat the eggs. Add coconut milk, melted coconut oil, honey, and vanilla extract. Mix well.
Add the wet ingredients to the dry ingredients and mix until smooth and well combined.
Divide the batter evenly among the cupcake liners.
Bake in the preheated oven for 18-22 minutes or until a toothpick inserted into the center comes out clean.
Allow the cupcakes to cool completely before frosting.
For the frosting, scoop the solid part of chilled coconut cream into a bowl, leaving any liquid behind. Add honey and vanilla extract. Whip until fluffy.
Frost the Vanilla Coconut Flour Cupcakes with the coconut cream frosting.
Optional: Garnish with shredded coconut or other toppings of your choice.

Enjoy these light and flavorful vanilla coconut flour cupcakes!

Sugar-Free Matcha Green Tea Ice Cream

Ingredients:

- 2 cans (27 ounces) full-fat coconut milk, chilled
- 2 tablespoons matcha green tea powder
- 1/2 cup powdered erythritol or any sugar substitute
- 1 teaspoon vanilla extract

Instructions:

Place the cans of coconut milk in the refrigerator for at least 8 hours or overnight to allow the cream to separate from the liquid.
Once chilled, carefully open the cans of coconut milk without shaking them. Scoop out the solid coconut cream into a bowl, leaving the liquid behind. You should have about 2 cups of coconut cream.
In a small bowl, mix the matcha green tea powder with a small amount of the coconut cream to create a smooth paste.
Add the matcha paste, powdered erythritol, and vanilla extract to the bowl of coconut cream. Whip the mixture until well combined and fluffy.
Transfer the mixture to an ice cream maker and churn according to the manufacturer's instructions until it reaches a soft-serve consistency.
If you don't have an ice cream maker, pour the mixture into a shallow dish and freeze. Every 30 minutes, stir the mixture with a fork to break up ice crystals until it reaches the desired consistency.
Once the Sugar-Free Matcha Green Tea Ice Cream is ready, transfer it to a lidded container and freeze for an additional 2-4 hours to firm up.
Before serving, let the ice cream sit at room temperature for a few minutes to soften slightly.
Scoop and enjoy this delightful and sugar-free matcha green tea treat!